Freestyle Skiing

by K. C. Kelley

Published by The Child's World®
1980 Lookout Drive
Mankato, MN 56003-1705
800-599-READ
www.childsworld.com

The Child's World®: Mary Berendes, Publishing Director
Shoreline Publishing Group, LLC: James Buckley Jr.,
  Production Director
The Design Lab: Design and production

ISBN: 978-1-60973-210-3
LCCN: 2011928881

Photo credits: Cover: Corbis.
Interior: AP/Wide World: 4, 8, 11, 12, 17, 23, 24;
dreamstime.com: Neil Harrison, 20; Julijah, 27;
Photos.com: 7, 15, 28

Printed in the United States of America
Mankato, Minnesota
July, 2011
PA02094

Table of Contents

Jeret Peterson celebrates after nailing his Hurricane jump.

CHAPTER ONE

Skiing . . . or Flying?

The Winter Olympic Games sometimes have blizzards. Big snowstorms are part of the fun at the winter sports event. In Vancouver in 2010, though, Jeret Peterson made a hurricane!

Peterson is a freestyle skier from Idaho. He is the only skier in the world to do a trick called the Hurricane. After flying up from a ramp, he flips three times and spins five times . . . before landing with a thump!

For several years, Peterson was great at the Hurricane in practice runs. But in events, he often fell during the landing. In 2010, on the world's biggest sports stage, he came through. As fans chanted his name, he flew through the air, spinning and twisting. He landed perfectly and the crowd screamed!

He got the highest score for any jump at that Olympics. Combined with his first jump, it gave him a silver medal for second place. The medal was great, of course. Landing his amazing Hurricane, however, gave him the greatest joy.

"For me to land this and earn a medal . . . I'm **stoked**!" he said afterward.

Freestyle skiing gives skiers like Peterson amazing ways to show off their skills. Some skiers early in the 1900s did some easy spins or small jumps. Olympic gold medalist Stein Eriksen from Sweden was the first to really do **aerial** (AIR-ee-uhl) tricks on skis in the 1950s. In the 1970s, ski gear became lighter and more flexible. Daring skiers tried more and more tricks on their skis. These skiers were known as "hot doggers."

Aerial skiers do tricks after making short jumps.

A steep ramp sends aerial skiers high into the air.

The first world championships were held in 1986. Two years later, the sports were **demonstrated** at the Winter Olympics in Calgary, Canada. In 1992, they became official medal sports; that means that the top three finishers got official gold, silver, and bronze Olympic medals.

Eventually, freestyle skiing grew into three main sports.

- Aerials: Skiers without ski poles slide down a short hill and then up into the air from a ramp. In the air, they perform spins, twists, and flips. Top skiers can fly as much as 50 to 60 feet (15 to 18 m) in the air after zooming off the ramp. They land on the slope below the ramp. Judges give them points for their skills in the air and for their landing.

• Moguls (MOH-guhls): A series of short, tightly-spaced bumps called moguls are carved on a snow-packed hillside. Skiers must move down the hill going over bump after bump. On most courses, there are also two smaller jumps. Judges are looking for perfect form, with knees together and hands pumping. Moguls skiers are also judged on how fast they can do the course.

Moguls skiers deal with bumps and short jumps like this one.

Skiers race very close together in skicross.

- Skicross: This is the newest freestyle skiing event. It joined the Olympics in 2010. Skiers race along a curving course with several jumps. Unlike other ski races, skiers race against each other, four at a time. In most ski races, skiers compete alone for the best times.

This book will focus mostly on aerial freestyle skiing.

Most skiing is done on the ground, along snow-covered hills and mountains. Aerial skiers take to the sky instead. They combine athletic skill with great bravery. Let's look up and check out aerial skiing!

CHAPTER TWO

Freestyle Basics

Aerial skiers use special types of skis. Regular racing skis have curved tips at the front end. They are square at the back. Most aerial skis have curved tips at the front and back of each ski. In some moves, skiers are going backward, so the tips at the back help keep the skis from crossing.

Their boots are much stiffer than those used in ski racing. The stiff sides help the aerial skier "**stick**" his or her landing. Racing boots have to be more flexible to allow for quick turns. Aerial skiers don't turn! Some aerial skiers have their boots custom-made to fit just their feet and no one else's.

Freestyle skiing boots provide great ankle support.

The white patches on this mogul skier's pants
help judges follow his knee movement.

For safety on landing, aerial skiers wear a hard plastic helmet. Depending on weather, they might also wear goggles. Since they're in a winter sport, they also wear gloves and full-body ski suits. These suits are made of material that keeps the skier warm and keeps water and snow out.

Mogul skiers also have special skis and boots. They also use long poles with spiked ends to help them move through their bouncy course. White patches on their knees stand out against their colored suits. The patches help judges more easily watch the skiers' form during the events.

With the gear ready, it's time to learn. Young skiers can't try aerials or moguls until they are very good at normal skiing. They begin their aerial training with very low jumps. They go off the jump and land without twisting or spinning. As they get better, they can add twists and spins.

Aerial skiers can also practice in two fun ways without snow. In the summer, they ski on hills and ramps covered with a special mat. When wet, the mat is as slick as snow. They land not on a hill . . . but in a swimming pool. They wear life jackets and swim trunks along with their helmets.

To practice their moves in the air, some aerial skiers use a trampoline. They train their bodies to flip, spin, and twist in the air. First they do it without skis. Then they can do the jumps on trampolines using smaller skis.

Splashdown ahead: This young skier will land in the pool after a practice jump.

This series shows the midair moves of a freestyle skier.

Once they are very well-trained, aerial skiers enter events. Judges in the events look for three things: air, form, and landing. For air, skiers get points for how high and far they jump. Form means how they hold and move their bodies throughout the run down the ramp and during the jump. Other judges watch the skiers land. These judges give marks for how well the skier sticks the landing (which means landing without falling or stumbling).

CHAPTER THREE

Freestyle Stars and Tricks

Aerial skiing stars come from all around the world. In 2010, Alexei Grishin (GREE-shin) of Belarus won the men's gold medal in aerials. Grishin got a terrific score on his second jump in Vancouver. He barely edged out American star Jeret Peterson and his Hurricane jump. Grishin's gold was the first ever for Belarus.

In the women's event, Lydia Lassila from far-off Australia was the winner. She was an upset winner over Li Nina from China. Guo Xinxin of China won the bronze in the event.

Alexei Grishin shows off his gold medal-winning form.

China's Xu Mengtao is one of the world's top aerial skiers.

China has become a world leader in the sport. Li won the 2010 World Cup championship. The World Cup is a long series of events. Skiers earn points from each event. The skier with the most points is the season's World Cup champ. In 2011, the top five World Cup women's aerial skiers were from China. Chinese men held the top two spots and three of the top four.

Canada, Ukraine, and Switzerland also are home to many top aerial skiers. Peterson is still one of the best American male aerial skiers.

All these skiers perform tricks with memorable names. A full spin is a 360. Two spins are a 720. In a backscratcher, the skier pulls the back of his skis so that they reach up behind his back. Any trick in which the skier reaches down to touch his skis is a grab. Other tricks are described by their parts, such as a double-twist, triple-flip. Whatever you call them, these tricks are amazing to watch!

A ski grab like this is one of many types of aerial tricks.

In other freestyle news, Canadian fans enjoyed watching their own Alexandre Bilodeau win the moguls gold medal in 2010. U.S. star Hannah Kearney took the gold in the women's event. Michael Schmid of Switzerland won the first men's skicross gold medal. Hometown hero Ashleigh McIvor of Canada won the women's event.

Bouncing over moguls or flying through the air, freestyle skiers are taking their sport to new heights and new directions. Look, up in the sky . . . it's a skier!

"New school" freestyle skiers include rails and other objects in their runs.

Glossary

aerial—in the air

demonstrated—showed others how something is done

elegant—beautiful and luxurious

hemisphere—half of a sphere; the Earth has two hemispheres.

stick—in skiing, to land solidly without stumbling or falling

stoked—slang word that means really excited

Find Out More

BOOKS

Alpine and Freestyle Skiing
By Kylie Burns. New York, NY: Crabtree, 2010.
From flying high off ramps to skiing down super-steep mountainsides,
this book takes you even further into the world of amazing skiers.

Skiing & Snowboarding: Girls Play to Win
By Karen L. Kenney. Chicago, IL: Norwood House Press, 2011.
This book includes information on freestyle skiing, as well as downhill
and other Olympic skiing sports. Highlights include a special section on
skiing history and biographies of top skiers.

WEB SITES

For links to learn more about extreme sports: **childsworld.com/links**

Note to Parents, Teachers, and Librarians: We routinely verify our Web
links to make sure they are safe and active sites. So encourage your
readers to check them out!

Index

About the Author

K. C. Kelley lives far away from the snow, but he is amazed watching freestyle skiers fly through the air. A longtime author of sports books for young readers, he has written about baseball, football, basketball, and soccer, as well as books about animals, astronauts, and other cool stuff.